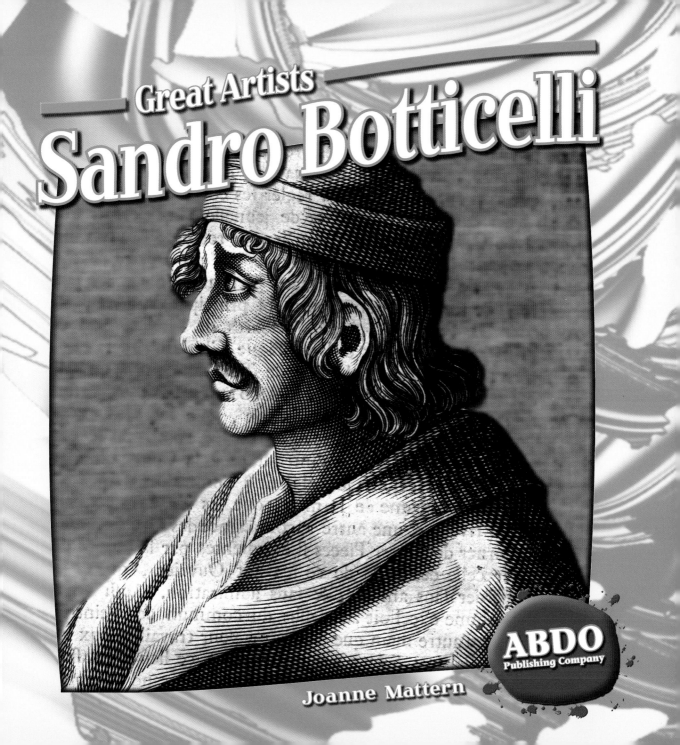

Great Artists

Sandro Botticelli

Joanne Mattern

ABDO
Publishing Company

visit us at
www.abdopub.com

Published by ABDO Publishing Company, 4940 Viking Drive, Edina, Minnesota 55435.
Copyright © 2005 by Abdo Consulting Group, Inc. International copyrights reserved in all
countries. No part of this book may be reproduced in any form without written permission
from the publisher. The Checkerboard Library™ is a trademark and logo of ABDO Publishing
Company.

Printed in the United States.

Cover Photo: Getty Images
Interior Photos: Bridgeman Art Library pp. 15, 25; Corbis pp. 8, 9, 11, 12, 13, 17, 19, 20, 21,
    23, 28, 29; Getty Images pp. 1, 5, 14, 26, 27; North Wind p. 10

Series Coordinator: Megan Murphy
Editors: Jennifer R. Krueger, Megan Murphy
Cover Design: Neil Klinepier
Interior Design: Dave Bullen

Library of Congress Cataloging-in-Publication Data

Mattern, Joanne, 1963-
    Sandro Botticelli / Joanne Mattern.
       p. cm. -- (Great artists)
    Includes index.
    ISBN 1-59197-839-4
    1. Botticelli, Sandro, 1444 or 5-1510--Juvenile literature. 2. Painters--Italy--Biography--
Juvenile literature. I. Title.

ND623.B7M38 2005
759.5--dc22
[B]
                                                                    2004052813

Contents

Sandro Botticelli

Sandro Botticelli was an artist who lived more than 550 years ago. He lived in the city of Florence, Italy. Florence was known for its beautiful artwork and the many artists who lived there.

Botticelli lived during the **Renaissance**. At that time, art and sculpture were very important to people. Many famous paintings and other works of art were created during the Renaissance.

Botticelli often showed his religious devotion in his work. He painted Jesus and Mary. Many churches in Florence displayed his work. Botticelli also painted figures from mythology. One of his most famous paintings is called *The Birth of Venus*.

Botticelli died in 1510. For a time, his work was nearly forgotten. However, it became popular again more than 300 years after he died. Today, Botticelli is considered one of the greatest Renaissance painters.

Botticelli's self-portrait from the painting Adoration of the Magi

Timeline

1444 or 1445 ~ Sandro Botticelli was born in Florence, Italy.

1461 or 1462 ~ Botticelli went to work in Fra Filippo Lippi's workshop.

1467 ~ Lippi left Florence.

1470 ~ Botticelli began working on his own; from June to August, Botticelli painted *Fortitude*.

1473 or 1474 ~ Botticelli was asked to paint *St. Sebastian* in Florence's Church of Santa Maria Maggiore.

1476 ~ A Florentine commissioned a painting called the *Adoration of the Magi*.

1477 ~ Botticelli was asked to paint *Primavera*.

1481 ~ Botticelli went to Rome at the request of Pope Sixtus IV. He painted several scenes from the Bible for the Sistine Chapel.

1482 ~ Botticelli returned to Florence.

1484 to 1486 ~ Botticelli painted *The Birth of Venus*.

1494 ~ The Medicis were driven out of Florence.

1510 ~ Botticelli died in Florence on May 17.

Late 1800s ~ A new interest in Botticelli's work emerged.

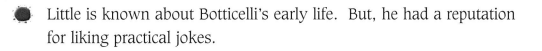

Fun Facts

 Not only was Botticelli called the Little Barrel, but some say his whole family was called that!

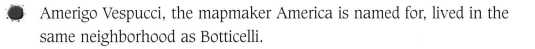 Little is known about Botticelli's early life. But, he had a reputation for liking practical jokes.

 Botticelli's father described the boy on a tax form as being a hard studier, but "sickly."

Amerigo Vespucci, the mapmaker America is named for, lived in the same neighborhood as Botticelli.

Botticelli's masterpieces now hang in museums. But some, such as *Primavera*, were originally painted to decorate the houses of his friends and employers.

 The first time Botticelli signed and dated a painting was in 1501 for the *Mystic Nativity*.

"The Little Barrel"

Sandro Botticelli was born in Florence, Italy, in 1444 or 1445. Botticelli was not his real name. His real name was Alessandro di Mariano Filipepi.

Botticelli was a nickname he got when he was young. Some people think this nickname came from Sandro's brother Giovanni. Giovanni was known as *Il Botticello*. This means "the little barrel" in Italian. Giovanni got this nickname because he was fat, like a barrel.

For some reason, people called Sandro that, too! Other historians think that Botticelli got his nickname a different way. When he was a teenager, he had a job pounding gold. A gold pounder was called a *battigello*. Over time, *battigello* became Botticelli.

Florence, Italy

This Florence street leads to the Santa Maria del Fiore, a cathedral built in the 1300s.

The Filipepis

Sandro's family lived a comfortable life. His father, Mariano di Vanni Filipepi, was a **tanner**. His mother was Smeralda Filipepi. The Filipepi family lived in an area of Florence called Santa Maria Novella. This neighborhood was near the Arno River.

Sandro had three older brothers. The oldest was Giovanni, who worked as a **pawnbroker**. The second brother was Antonio, a **goldsmith**. The third brother was Simone. Simone spent most of his life as a trader in Naples, Italy.

All of Sandro's brothers had very good careers. They were all healthy and successful, too. But, Sandro was pale and thin. He was sick many times during his childhood.

Simone was a trader on the Mediterranean like the men in this woodcut.

The Arno River flows for 150 miles (241 km) through Italy.

As a boy, Sandro spent much of his time drawing. Mariano thought his son should settle down in a job. However, Sandro did not know what he wanted to do for a living.

The Apprentice

Sandro knew his father wanted him to get a job. So, Sandro went to work for his brother Antonio, the **goldsmith**, as an apprentice.

An apprentice was a boy who worked for someone else to learn a trade. Apprentices did a lot of hard work. They did not get paid. Instead, they received food and a place to sleep. When an apprentice had learned the business, he started working on his own.

But, Sandro did not want to be a goldsmith. He realized he loved art. At his brother's shop, he met many painters and other artists. Soon, Sandro knew what he wanted to do with his life. He told Mariano he wanted to be a painter.

A modern goldsmith in Florence, Italy, practices his craft.

Sandro was older than many apprentices,
and his talent set him apart from the rest.

Fra Filippo Lippi

Mariano agreed that his son could be an artist. He found a position for Sandro. Sandro would be an apprentice to the painter Fra Filippo Lippi.

Lippi was one of the finest artists in Florence. He painted many religious works. Lippi had great influence on Sandro's paintings.

In 1461 or 1462, Sandro went to work in Lippi's workshop. Sandro was about 16 years old when he became Lippi's apprentice. Most apprentices were younger than he was. However, Sandro did not let his age stop him from learning. He worked very hard.

Fra Filippo Lippi

Botticelli's **Madonna of the Sea** (left) *is similar to* **Madonna and Child** (right) *painted by Lippi.*

At first, Lippi only allowed Sandro to mix paint and do small tasks. These jobs were not very exciting. But, they taught Sandro many things about being an artist.

Sandro also had the chance to watch Lippi work. When Sandro got older, Lippi allowed him to help with some of his paintings. In many of Sandro's early paintings, Lippi's influence can be seen in color, **perspective**, and graceful clothing.

Art Lessons

In 1467, Lippi left Florence. He went to work in Spoleto, Italy. Botticelli stayed in Florence. He worked for other painters. These painters were brothers, Piero and Antonio Pollaiuolo.

The Pollaiuolo brothers had a different style from Lippi. They were naturalists. Naturalists believed that art should be realistic. They used science and research to create paintings.

Botticelli learned many things from these painters. He learned more about **perspective**. He also studied how the human body moved. He learned how to show these movements in his paintings.

Botticelli was also influenced around this time by a painter named Andrea del Verrocchio. Botticelli was developing his own style based on Verrocchio's work and on the work of the Pollaiuolo brothers. This style included graceful figures, a grasp of perspective, and the use of pale colors.

Another artist who was influenced by Verrocchio was Leonardo da Vinci. When Leonardo was 15, he became an apprentice in Verrocchio's workshop.

The Medicis

Botticelli started working on his own around 1470. He was about 25 years old. It didn't take long for him to get his first **commission**.

The Pollaiuolo brothers were asked to create a series of paintings. These paintings would hang in a courtroom that settled disputes between merchants. The Pollaiuolos asked Botticelli to complete one of the paintings. It was called *Fortitude*.

Botticelli worked on *Fortitude* between June 18 and August 18, 1470. The painting was a huge success. But, Botticelli had more important friends to give him commissions.

The Medici family ruled Florence at that time. Lorenzo de Medici was the head of the family. He became Botticelli's patron. He showed Botticelli's work to his friends. Many important people in Florence started asking Botticelli to work for them. He soon became one of the most popular artists in Florence.

A statue of Lorenzo de Medici by the artist Michelangelo

Religious Works

Botticelli created many religious works during his lifetime. In 1473 or 1474, he was **commissioned** to paint *St. Sebastian* in Florence's Church of Santa Maria Maggiore.

In about 1476, a Florentine commissioned a painting called the *Adoration of the Magi*. This became one of Botticelli's most famous works. The painting shows many people coming to see the baby Jesus.

Botticelli liked to include his friends in his paintings. Members of the Medici family are pictured in the *Adoration of the Magi*. Botticelli is in the picture, too. He is the young man in yellow at the far right side of the picture.

Roman soldiers tried to kill Saint Sebastian by tying him to a tree and shooting him with arrows. But, he lived!

🔴 Lorenzo the Magnificent   🔴 Giuliano de Medici

🔴 Commissioner of the painting   🔴 Botticelli

The patronage of a wealthy family was very important to Botticelli and all artists working during his time. Wealthy families bought art and built the reputation of an artist. Botticelli's display of the Medicis in the Adoration of the Magi *shows how important this culture of patronage was to Botticelli. Today, the* Adoration of the Magi *hangs in Florence's Uffizi Gallery.*

Primavera

In addition to religious works, Botticelli also painted scenes using figures from mythology. In 1477, Lorenzo de Medici asked Botticelli to paint a scene of springtime. He created a work called *Primavera*.

Primavera is the Italian word for spring. Botticelli's *Primavera* includes Venus, who was the Roman goddess of love and beauty. Cupid flies over Venus's head. Cupid is another figure from Roman mythology. He shoots arrows to make people fall in love.

The painting also includes Flora, the goddess of springtime. She is spreading flowers across the scene. All the figures are in a wood filled with fruit trees. These trees celebrate the richness of springtime.

Primavera was a huge success. Botticelli was honored by members of Lorenzo de Medici's court. He was one of the most famous and respected artists in Florence. Soon, he would have the chance to take his talents to even greater places.

Artist's Corner

Many aspects of Botticelli's *Primavera* show his unique style, as well as the style of Renaissance painters in general. Parts of this style include color, perspective, and subject. Botticelli used pale colors, such as the blue of Venus's dress or the flesh tones of the Three Graces on the left.

Botticelli also uses perspective in a way that was important to Renaissance painters. The figures are in the foreground, while the wood gives the background. This creates the illusion of depth that was perfected by Renaissance painters.

Other details of *Primavera* are also classic elements of Botticelli's style. These include the melancholy looks on the subjects' faces, as well as the way their bodies appear to move gracefully.

Off to Rome

Until 1481, Botticelli spent his entire life in Florence. That year, he went to Rome at the request of Pope Sixtus IV. The Sistine Chapel had recently been completed. The pope invited several of Italy's most famous artists to paint **frescoes** on the walls of the new chapel.

Botticelli painted several frescoes for the Sistine Chapel. They were called *Life of Moses*, *Temptation of Christ*, and *Punishment of Korah*. These paintings show scenes from the Bible. These works are related to each other and to other works of art in the chapel.

It was a big challenge for Botticelli to work with other artists. But, he finished painting the scenes in less than 11 months! It was a huge accomplishment. Botticelli returned to Florence in 1482. Soon, he would create his most famous masterpiece.

Botticelli's Sistine Chapel paintings,
such as Temptation of Christ (top) *and* Life of
Moses (bottom), *show his religious devotion.*

Birth of Venus

Botticelli's time in Rome only allowed his reputation to grow. Botticelli created many religious paintings after his return to Florence. He created several small paintings for residences, too. He needed the help of artists in his workshop just to finish his **commissions**!

From 1484 to 1486, he created a painting called *The Birth of Venus*. Like many of his other works, this painting was probably commissioned by the Medici family.

The Birth of Venus features the Roman goddess Venus. This is the same goddess shown in *Primavera*. The painting shows the goddess standing on a seashell. She is being blown to shore by the wind. *The Birth of Venus* is one of the most famous paintings in the world.

A worker in Florence, Italy, prepares for an exhibition of Botticelli's work.

The Roman goddess Venus was said to have risen from the sea. The Birth of Venus reflects that myth.

Later Years

By 1491, Botticelli was one of the most powerful artists in Florence. He was a busy and important man. There is no record that Botticelli ever married or had a family. The most important things in his life were his art and his religion. Botticelli's style showed his deepening religious devotion.

In the 1490s, a monk named Girolamo Savonarola gained power in Florence. Savonarola thought the lifestyle of the Medicis was too **materialistic**. The Medicis were driven out of Florence in 1494.

By the early 1500s, people were looking for a new kind of art. Botticelli's work was not popular anymore. He died in Florence on May 17, 1510. He was 65 years old. Botticelli was buried at the Church of the Ognissanti in Florence.

A statue of Girolamo Savonarola

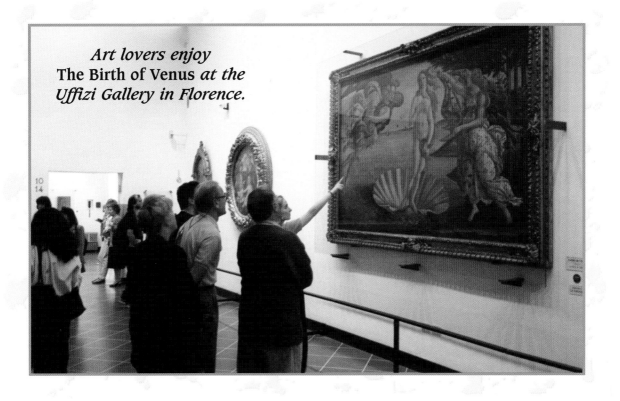

Art lovers enjoy **The Birth of Venus** *at the Uffizi Gallery in Florence.*

For a time, Botticelli and his work were forgotten. Then, a group of artists rediscovered him during the late 1800s. These artists were called the **Pre-Raphaelites**. The Pre-Raphaelites admired the way Botticelli painted.

Today, Sandro Botticelli's paintings hang in famous museums. These include the Louvre in Paris, the National Gallery of Art in Washington, D.C., and the Metropolitan Museum of Art in New York City. Even though he painted more than 500 years ago, Botticelli's works are still enjoyed today.

Glossary

commission - a request to complete a work, such as a painting, for a certain person. To be commissioned is to be given such a request.

fresco - the art of painting on a wet surface that becomes hard when dry, such as a plaster wall.

goldsmith - a person who works with gold.

materialistic - of or relating to the belief that the greatest value of life is based on owning items of value or importance.

pawnbroker - a person who lends money in exchange for personal property.

perspective - the art of giving objects drawn on a flat surface the illusion of being three-dimensional.

Pre-Raphaelites - a group of artists in England working in 1848 to restore the ideas and practices of fifteenth century Italian art.

Renaissance - a revival of art and learning that began in Italy during the fourteenth century, marked by a renewed interest in Greek and Latin literature and art.

tan - to make a hide into leather by soaking it in a special liquid. A person who does this is a tanner.

Saying It

Filipepi – fee-lee-PAH-pee
Filippo Lippi – fee-LEEP-poh LEEP-pee
Girolamo Savonarola – jee-RAW-lahm-oh sah-voh-nah-RAW-lah
Medici – MEHD-ee-chee
Piero Pollaiuolo – PYAY-roh pohl-leye-WAW-loh
Renaissance – reh-nuh-SAHNS
Sixtus – SIHK-stuhs

Web Sites

To learn more about Sandro Botticelli, visit ABDO Publishing Company on the World Wide Web at **www.abdopub.com**. Web sites about Botticelli are featured on our Book Links page. These links are routinely monitored and updated to provide the most current information available.

Index